Ignoramus

IGNORAMUS
a play by James Reaney

Vancouver, Talonbooks, 1978

published with assistance from the Canada Council

Talonbooks
201 1019 East Cordova
Vancouver
British Columbia V6A 1M8
Canada

This book was typeset by Linda Gilbert of B.C. Monthly Typesetting Service, designed by David Robinson and printed by Hemlock Printers for Talonbooks.

First printing: December 1978

Talonplays are edited by Peter Hay.

Canadian Cataloguing in Publication Data

   Reaney, James, 1926-
   Ignoramus

   ISBN 0-88922-155-3

   I. Title.
   PS8535.E295I4   jC812'.5'4   C79-091078-0
   PR9199.3.R425I4

Introduction

Some time ago over **CBC** *Wednesday Night* I remember hearing a wonderful debate between Dr. Hilda Neatby and somebody else about her book, *So Little for the Mind*. The controversy about educational theory that arose from this book in the early fifties brought out tensions and groupings still visible, no matter how changed.

More or less as a tribute to that debate I have written *Ignoramus*. I have always wanted to try an Aristophanes Old Comedy type of play where you have lots of comic chorus work and grotesque farcical combats. Also, this is a companion play to *Names and Nicknames*: there I used an old public-school text — *The Practical Speller*; here I have used *Cours Moyen* and other high-school texts so that it can easily be a play for young people with their teachers taking the adult roles, all working together at interpretation and precision. I hope the play is amusing, but also I hope that if you saw the Roman Empire as a chant-dance-mime in front of you, you might then take away the attitude that history was fun, not just labour. Similarly with the grammar scene and the chemistry sequence. A whole school and all its curricular and extra-curricular activities can be involved. One production used the swim team as the twenty orphan babes wheeled from the back of the cafeteria in shopping carts. The only caution with expansion of the script is that the pace and line of the play *must* be kept; there's no point in doing the chemistry, French or geometry sequences unless you can make them funny or dazzling or weird, but *always* part of the line forward. Bon Ami cans have changed, by the way. Find out from parents what they used to be like.

James Reaney
London, Ontario
December, 1973

Ignoramus was first performed at York Mills Collegiate Institute in Toronto, Ontario, in February, 1967, with the following cast:

Newsboy	David Marmorek
Announcer	Elliot Strom
Voices	Janet Goforth
Governor-General	Gordon Gates
Mr. Frothingale	John Porter
Dr. Hilda History	Brigitte Berman
Dr. Charles Progressaurus	Andy Stoddart, Graham Mackey
Beatrice	Taranch Harari, Martha Meschino
Bruce	Scott McGill
Cynthia	Pam Wiggin, Heather Gold
Stephen	Dean Samaris, Tony Hall
Dr. History's Pupils	Barbara Taylor, Marina Strauss
	Chris Schoeck, Gordon Thompson
	Judy Libman, David Marmorek
Dr. Progressaurus' Pupils	Helen Gibson, Sandra Feldman
	Bob Dolman, Jeff Gold
	Miriam Gotlib, Florence Minz
	Carol Duncan
Cheerleaders	Helen Meschino, Phil Holzberg
	Penny Tibbles. Carolyn Brown
	Bev Read, Jay Bigelow

Nurses and Babies	Wendy Clare, Jack Pasht
	Gail Stover, Dave Patterson
	Bill Pepall, Debbie Brooker
	Debbie Pemberton, Mark Shriver
	Sandy Imrie, Graham Clow
	Sue Fitzgerald, Charlie Lumbers
	Joyce Beaupre, Dave Shalof
	Pat Mackie, George Goldsmith
	Janet Goldring, John Baird
	Penny Luke, Bruce Grantier
	Johanne Clare, Tris Organ

Directed by Doug Dales
With the assistance of Mr. D. Daniels and Mr. R. Lawrason
Produced by Mr. D. Mogan with Howard Greenspan
and Kirk Hewitt
Costumes under the direction of Mrs. Don Lang
Music under the direction of Mr. Patterson

LIST OF CHARACTERS

NEWSBOY.
ANNOUNCER.
DR. HILDA HISTORY.
DR. CHARLES PROGRESSAURUS.
FIRST VOICE FROM THE AUDIENCE.
SECOND VOICE FROM THE AUDIENCE.
MR. FROTHINGALE, *a brewer.*
ALFRED, JERRY, BRUNO, STEPHEN, CYNTHIA,
    MARK, SAMUEL, DAVID AND OTHERS, *the
    children at Dr. History's school.*
BEATRICE, RALPH, MILDRED, BRUCE, BOB AND
    OTHERS, *the children at Dr. Progressaurus' school.*
THE GOVERNOR-GENERAL.

A bare, fully lit, uncurtained stage. There is a semi-circle of chairs with a janitor's broom leaning against one chair. As the play opens, a NEWSBOY comes screaming up the aisle, yelling the latest newspaper headline.

NEWSBOY: TWENTY ORPHANS AGED TWENTY
MONTHS MADE HOMELESS BY FLOOD. READ ALL
ABOUT IT. ORPHANAGE COLLAPSES. TWENTY
INFANT ORPHANS HOMELESS ON THE STREETS!

As his voice dies away, the actors in the play file onstage. Generally speaking there will be four actors for the adult parts and twenty actors for the student parts. All the actors should be prepared to fill in where necessary. That is, if nurses are needed for the school sequence, let someone don a nurse's blue cloak.

Marvin Mellowbell, Rawhide's ANNOUNCER, picks up the janitor's broom which has a CBC pinned on it and so we have a radio broadcast. Perhaps a box can be placed in front of him and two LISTENERS crouch at it twiddling with the knobs, adjusting their rocking chairs as he says . . .

ANNOUNCER: Good evening, ladies and gentlemen. This evening Citizen's Forum brings you a debate between . . . *There is a pause.*   DR. HILDA HISTORY who has just written a controversial book . . . *There is a pause.* *So Little for the Spine* — a debate between DR. HILDA HISTORY and, on the other hand, DR. CHARLES PROGRESSAURUS, B.A., M.A. Toronto, B. Paed. Toronto, D. Paed. Columb., principal of Toronto's famed Centre for Tomorrow's Education. DR. PROGRESSAURUS. Perhaps there are a few questions you would like to ask DR. HILDA HISTORY about her recent book *So Little for the Spine*. Now, some commentators have stated that it made the most crushing indictment possible of Centre for Tomorrow's Education and all progressive education.

DR. PROGRESSAURUS: It — *So Little for the Spine* — tried to make a crushing statement.

DR. HISTORY: It indicted and it crushed.

DR. HISTORY AND DR. PROGRESSAURUS:
Crush and Crunch
Gentle press
Crush!
Press!

They repeat these words until they become "Cress" and "Pruch."

DR. PROGRESSAURUS: Awgyh! You have written the most old-fashioned book. In which you say. That progressive education. Does not train the child's mind for anything.

DR. HISTORY: Right!

DR. PROGRESSAURUS: Ho ho ho! What's the use of training and straining and stuffing the child's mind with a lot of facts he'll never use. At Centre for Tomorrow's Education we believe in teaching the whole child to be happy, teaching him to fit into his environment — our great happy democracy.

DR. HISTORY: Define your terms! What do you mean by democracy?

DR. PROGRESSAURUS: I uh uh er would rather not say. With your very clever debating type mind you'd just — jump me.

DR. HISTORY: Oh ha! So you can't define, can't or won't define democracy and yet you're training the child to fit in with some great happy form of it. Dr. Progressaurus. Do you know what you're like?

DR. PROGRESSAURUS: *fascinated*   No. What am I like?

DR. HISTORY: You're like a man hammering a nail in the dark.

DR. PROGRESSAURUS: I suppose you believe in stuffing their minds with dates and figures and rules and theorems and — LATIN. Greek and LATIN.

DR. HISTORY: You're giving them something to think about. Latin trains the mind. LATIN.

DR. PROGRESSAURUS:
Latin
Is
Coffin Satin
Lining
So far as I'm concerned.

What I believe is that the child should be taught to express himself — just a moment, please let me finish, let me finish to express himself and to be happy in his environment.

DR. HISTORY: First of all: How can a child express himself if he's got nothing to express?

DR. PROGRESSAURUS: The self. Teach him to free the beautiful self!

DR. HISTORY: Perhaps he won't want to be happy in this society. Perhaps he'll decide that it's an evil society.

DR. PROGRESSAURUS: Oh he'll never say that about our free happy car-driving democracy.

DR. HISTORY: GRAMMAR helps one to speak!

DR. PROGRESSAURUS: BARE SUBJECT, BARE Slimubject. No child should be forced to learn what he doesn't want to learn.

DR. HISTORY: But how does he know that he doesn't want to until he's learned it?

DR. PROGRESSAURUS: It's too late then.

DR. HISTORY: Well, a little learning may be a dangerous thing, Dr. Progressaurus, but no learning at all should certainly be even more lethal.

DR. PROGRESSAURUS: You're not democratic.

DR. HISTORY: The mind is a kingdom. Surely the best democracies had lots of trained minds.

DR. PROGRESSAURUS: Aw — a telephone directory trains the mind. Driving a car trains the mind.

DR. HISTORY: With another five years of you around this country's schools our children will soon be able to read only traffic signals.

DR. PROGRESSAURUS: You are rather conventional in your views, but I think you will soon realize that you are attacking a good thing. Have you ever thought of the helpless misery your system inflicts on a child who can't parse a sentence or solve a problem in mathematics.

DR. HISTORY: Boo hoo!

ANNOUNCER: Ah — a question from the floor.

A VOICE: *from the audience*   I should like to ask Dr. History where she got the information for her book on modern education in the schools of tomorrow.

DR. HISTORY: My dear, the various provincial Departments of Education put out statements of what they're trying to do. It's usually what he says — train the child to fit in with our happy democracy and learn how to express himself. I beg your pardon?

THE VOICE FROM THE AUDIENCE: Uh — I was just going to add that I am a teacher and I never pay any attention to the curriculum the Department sends out.

DR. HISTORY: Good! I'm glad to hear it.

A SECOND VOICE: *from the audience*   I would like to ask Dr. Progressaurus if there isn't a problem about this fitting people into an environment.

DR. PROGRESSAURUS: My good man, what is your little problem?

THE SECOND VOICE FROM THE AUDIENCE: Suppose your environment's evil?

DR. PROGRESSAURUS: *sputtering*   But — you uh uh. In short, you believe the child is ignorant and imperfect and needs cultivation with dead language and so-called mental discipline?

DR. HISTORY: Yes. In short, you believe that the child is perfect and all his teacher should do is let him do what he likes. Good gracious me, that's how the Nazis trained their very best SS men. Just let them express themselves and Original Sin will do the rest! FIGHT!

They fence with huge cardboard swords.

STUDENTS: *onstage, taking sides and shouting*
Truth	Beauty	Kill him!
Self	Ex!	Pression!
Plato	Rousseau	Aristotle
Genesis	Abel	Cain!

Dr. HISTORY wins the fencing match just as the ANNOUNCER rings the bell.

ANNOUNCER: This is CBC's Citizen's Forum. In just ten seconds we'll give you the second round of the debate between Traditional and Modern, Old Fashioned and Progressive E-du-cation.

The STUDENTS divide into two groups — DR. HISTORY'S STUDENTS and DR. PROGRESSAURUS' STUDENTS.

DR. HISTORY'S STUDENTS: Dr. Hilda History said:

DR. HISTORY: I choose as my weapon — readers! Let us fight with readers, Dr. Progressaurus. Name the reader you would present to the infant unable to read.

DR. PROGRESSAURUS' STUDENTS: Dr. Progressaurus replied:

DR. PROGRESSAURUS: Dick, Jane and Puff. You name your reader.

DR. HISTORY'S STUDENTS: Dr. Hilda History replied:

DR. HISTORY: My primer reader for the infant Canadian shall be called — Julius Caesar, Cleopatra and Hannibal's Elephants.

DR. PROGRESSAURUS' STUDENTS: Dr. Progressaurus countered — rather weakly.

DR. PROGRESSAURUS: Well, I think that a little first book for a first little mind should have a little tittle — er, I mean, a little title: Mary, John and Peter?

DR. HISTORY'S STUDENTS: To which Dr. Hilda History said:

DR. HISTORY: My first reader is called: Eloise, Vercingetorix and Saint Peter.

DR. PROGRESSAURUS' STUDENTS: *BUT*, said Progressaurus:

DR. PROGRESSAURUS: You can't have a child's first
    reader called — that.

DR. HISTORY: Well, you can!

DR. HISTORY'S STUDENTS: She said she could!

DR. HISTORY: It's a duel to the death, Progressaurus.
    Let's throw our readers at each other.

*There is some sort of "discus-throwing" here with empty
boxes made to look like books. DR. HISTORY's reader
knocks DR. PROGRESSAURUS over.*

DR. HISTORY'S STUDENTS:
    She did. He did. Hers was so heavy, it knocked him
        down.
    And the citizens cheered.
    Hurrah for Grammar, Arithmetic, Logic.
    Down with Self-expression!

*Confetti and streamers are thrown here at DR. HISTORY,
who stands with her reader over the prostrate form of DR.
PROGRESSAURUS.*

*MR. FROTHINGALE, a wealthy brewer, now enters or
comes upon stage.*

MR. FROTHINGALE: Excuse me. But, Dr. History and
    Dr. Progressaurus, I've enjoyed this Citizen's Forum very
    much and I wondered if there was anything I could do
    to help.

DR. HISTORY: The Lord hath delivered mine enemy into
    my hands. What need I your help, merchant?

MR. FROTHINGALE: To find out. If you're right. On
the right track, you know. You see, I've simply pots —
really barrels of money to give away and nobody,
nobody, will take it.

DR. HISTORY: Goodness gracious me. Why won't they,
sir. Is your money tainted in some way?

MR. FROTHINGALE: The colleges won't touch it
because I simply asked that they call one of the buildings
I gave them Frothingale Hall. As you may know I'm a
very wealthy brewer.

DR. HISTORY: Poor little rich brewer, eh? I'm afraid,
my dear fellow, I still don't see how you can help us.

MR. FROTHINGALE: Well. I just happen to have
adopted twenty orphans. Suppose, let us suppose, that
with my millions of hiccup money I were to build you
each a school — a small village even, in some remote part
of the country, and you each with ten children apiece
were to find out over a period of say seventeen years,
were to find out just what happens when you Dr. Hilda
History bring up kids according to your traditional
methods and you, Dr. Progressaurus use your progressive
theories on your ten little younkers.

DR. PROGRESSAURUS: *rising*   I'll win this debate
yet. You'll see — give me a chance to educate the whole
child and in seventeen years I'll turn out paragons!

DR. HISTORY: Where are the infants? I'm game,
Frothingale.

MR. FROTHINGALE: I've got them just outside. Earlier this evening their orphanage was flooded out and poor little dears, I took them in at the Frothingale Brewery. But do wait. There is a catch. At the end of the seventeen year period — Grade Twelve or Middle School, as it used to be called in my very old fashioned youth, then we will meet again and a judge chosen by me will decide — which one of you wins. I'll have him see your children — why, they'll be almost grown up then.

DR. HISTORY: What do the children get out of this? Besides our experimenting with them. By the way, Frothingale, you must somehow arrange that they have foster parents immediately. I don't want them to grow up thinking *I'm* their mother.

MR. FROTHINGALE: I'll arrange that. When they are seventeen the children will get further board and tuition at whatever they want right up to the Ph.D. But the group that wins will inherit — the Frothingale Brewery, and I might say that means a great deal of hic-cup money. I have no children. My wealth embarrasses me. Forge me a society of human beings who will know what to do with my money when I'm gone.

DR. HISTORY AND DR. PROGRESSAURUS: Bring forth the orphans!

The STUDENTS who have retired now come on wheeling empty baby carriages. They are both nurses and babies. The babies gurgle, coo and cry and reach for comfort. Let the image register of twenty orphan babies, THEN . . .

DR. PROGRESSAURUS: Are we allowed to choose our
ten babies? Hey, Dr. History, stop. She's picking out
the pippins. I'll have this one. Heavens! Look what a
temper it has! Why it's getting redder and redder in
the face. Perhaps I'd — he looks like a smart little duffer
— Ughhh! He bit my finger!

MR. FROTHINGALE: No, you are neither of you
allowed to choose. If you'll notice, there is a number
on each carriage, duplicated, by a number in a medallion
linked around each little dimpled wrist — you must close
your eyes and choose the numbers from — my hat.

He shuffles the numbers in the hat and then presents it to
DR. HISTORY and DR. PROGRESSAURUS.

DR. HISTORY: Ah, 9! Oh, goodness me, number 7.
The one that found your finger so tasty, Progressaurus.

DR. PROGRESSAURUS: Ah 12. Look at those eyes.
Good heavens! Hasn't he rather a lot of teeth for two
months?

MR. FROTHINGALE: Tomorrow you will each take
your ten infants to opposite ends of Canada. You, Dr.
Progressaurus, on an island in Lake Erie where arrangements will be made. You, Dr. History, in a remote prairie
village where arrangements will be made. Tell me what
you want. Your wish is my command.

DR. HISTORY: Nurses! Babies 9, 7, 2, 5, 11, 13, 15,
16, 18, 20 are to be put to bed this very minute. I suggest
a two o'clock feeding which I will personally prepare.
Number 2 here is sucking his little big toe. I don't think
that is a good thing. Suppose we paint it with ipecacuanha.
Then . . .   *They fade off*   . . . the little dear will get
the idea.

DR. PROGRESSAURUS: Well, Nurse. What do babies
feel like doing at this hour of night? Do you want to go
to sleep? Or stay up and play?

*One baby, as his ten are wheeled out and he follows, utters
a blood curdling baby shriek!*

*MR. FROTHINGALE advances towards the audience and
confides in them.*

MR. FROTHINGALE: And so, near Dauphin, Manitoba,
Dr. Hilda History reared her brood of ten. And so, on
Pelee Island, in Lake Erie, Dr. Progressaurus reared his
brood of ten. You must imagine now that six years pass
and the earth turning and turning we come to Dr.
Hilda History's classroom first, though of course I only
heard of this many years later.

*Perhaps he stands at the edge of the stage whirling a globe
and looking on.*

*DR. HISTORY enters with her little scholars. They sit in a
circle and hear the end of the fairy tale, "Rapunzel."*

CHILD: Please Miss History, I'm afraid of the dark at
night. What can I do about being afraid of he dark?

DR. HISTORY: Be afraid of it. If you're afraid of it now
you won't be afraid of it later.

CHILD: Should we be afraid of the dark?

DR. HISTORY: Yes. The dark *is* frightening. I'm still
afraid of it, somewhat. But, child, once you see that it is
frightening, then it's no longer quite so frightening, is it?

CHILD: My father says you shouldn't read us stories about big giant people like Hercules.

DR. HISTORY: And why not, if I may ask?

CHILD: He says it will give me an inferiority complex.

DR. HISTORY: You tell your father, child, that at this stage you should have an inferiority complex. Will you tell him that?

CHILD: Yes, Miss History. Miss History, my mother told me last night in the village that we had not always lived here, but came from ever so many miles away all as babies on the train.

DR. HISTORY: Yes. I think everyone in the village remembers that night. In good time I will tell you why we are here.

CHILD: Are you God, Miss History?

DR. HISTORY: No, dear. I'm not.

CHILD: That's what the people in the village call you.

DR. HISTORY: Yes, that fact has percolated through to me.

CHILD: Are you our real mother, Miss History?

DR. HISTORY: My dear child, no. Ah, those fingernails are clean today. Now you may put away your embroidery girls, and boys, be careful of your needle when folding up your darning.

CHILD: Miss History, who are our real fathers and mothers?

DR. HISTORY: We can never know, dear. But your foster
    mothers and foster fathers in the village love you just as
    dearly. Why the stars are coming out and it's only four
    o'clock in the afternoon. I must say we were sent to a
    village sufficiently remote. Put on your overshoes and
    we'll race back to the village. See how many constellations
    you can name.

*They mime putting on overshoes and the journey into
the village. Perhaps they carry flashlights.*

DR. HISTORY'S STUDENTS:

Cassiopeia's Chair	The Dipper	The Pleiades
The Hare	Orion	Perseus
Pegasus	Ursa Major	Ursa Minor
The Dragon.		

DR. HISTORY: Excellent. Now see how many individual
    stars you can call by name.

CHILD: Oh look, Miss History. There's the lights of the
    village. Don't they look like stars?

DR. HISTORY and her STUDENTS exit.

*DR. PROGRESSAURUS comes on with his brood. He is just
finishing up the story of "The Little Blue Engine." — "He
thought he could. He thought he could. And so the milk,
the toys, the apples and the oranges* did *get to the good
little boys and girls on the other side of the mountain."*

BEATRICE: Dr. Progressaurus, could you tell us a fairy
    tale?

DR. PROGRESSAURUS: Tell you a what? Wherever did
    you hear about fairy tales?

CHILD: The nurse told Alice one last night when she couldn't sleep. It was lovely. All about a girl who had hair so long it could be used for a ladder.

DR. PROGRESSAURUS: Beatrice, don't you see the harm it might do you? Why all sorts of dreadful things happen in that story that would — oh just unsettle your little mind. You might get an inferiority complex and want your hair to be long, long, long.

BEATRICE: But we're not jealous of the little blue engine.

DR. PROGRESSAURUS: All right. I'll change the part where the rustly old engine can't get over the mountain. I didn't know you saw yourself that way.

BEATRICE: But Dr. Progressaurus I *want* you to tell me a fairy tale.

DR. PROGRESSAURUS: You can't truly want that, dear. Let's put it to a vote then.

BEATRICE: No, no, no. Please don't, Dr. Progressaurus.

DR. PROGRESSAURUS: Why don't you call me by my first name, Beatrice? Eh? If I told you a fairy tale it would ruin your vocabularies. You all know exactly one hundred words. And I'd have to do a word count on a fairy tale before I could read it to you. Now, kids, now that our story's over, let us do some finger painting.

They mime this.

CHILD: Hey, Charley. I'm afraid of the dark at night.

DR. PROGRESSAURUS: Ask Nursey to leave your light on, Ralph.

CHILD: Charley, why am I afraid of the dark?

DR. PROGRESSAURUS: It's a complex you've got, kid. But there's a nice old man coming here on Friday night and he'll find out why you're afraid of the dark.

BEATRICE: Isn't he afraid of the dark because it's dark?

DR. PROGRESSAURUS: Beatrice. Get your hands into the paint more, dear. Why golly, little man, don't you want to finger paint?

CHILD: *razzberrying*   Nah. I hates finger-painting.

DR. PROGRESSAURUS: *taking notes*   But all the other kiddies are loving their finger painting.

CHILD: Nah. I hates it, Charley. I don't want to.

DR. PROGRESSAURUS: Well, Jerry. *Don't* you finger paint. Don't you let me see you finger painting ever again.

The CHILD immediately digs into the paint pot and mimes a slather. DR. PROGRESSAURUS smiles benignly and passes on to the next CHILD. He picks up a small blanket.

DR. PROGRESSAURUS: I say, Mildred. What is this blanket you're always carrying around?

CHILD: It's my beddie. Don't you dare touch it.

DR. PROGRESSAURUS: My dear little girl, all the other children don't have to have their beddy blankets with them.

CHILD: Well, I do. And you leave it alone, Charles.

BEATRICE: You have your pipe, Dr. Progressaurus. If you're going to ask that Mildred give up her beddy then you should give up your old pipe.

DR. PROGRESSAURUS: Mildred doesn't have to give it up, Beatrice. Golly, for a six year old girl you're — a regular caution. Now, kids. If you like, go over and wash your hands and then lie down on your mattresses for the resting time.

They mime washing up, splashing and lying down.

BEATRICE: *drying her hands*   Dr. Progressaurus. Why do we live in a place that's all alone except for you and the nurses? Have we always been here?

DR. PROGRESSAURUS: No. You're part of a wonderful experiment, Beatrice.

BEATRICE: You're not our father then?

DR. PROGRESSAURUS: No, dear.

BEATRICE: I didn't think you were. The kids were all talking about this yesterday and some of them said the big tulip tree at the end of the garden was our father. You know the tree where the eagles nest?

DR. PROGRESSAURUS: No. I don't know. Now — if you like, *all* rest. Down on your matsies.   *Eventually they subside.*   I'll be down by the beach children if you need me. Smoking my beddy.

DR. PROGRESSAURUS exits.

BEATRICE: *rousing the sleeping forms* Come on, kids. I've got great news.

DR. PROGRESSAURUS' STUDENTS: What?!

BEATRICE: I've been learning how to read.

CHILD: Oh don't Beatrice. Charley says you'll go blind. Your eye-muscles aren't ready yet.

BEATRICE: I don't care. The farmer's wife taught me. They throw all their old tin cans across the fence into the school property in the woods. And I asked her if I could have one of the old tin cans with pictures on it and she said, "Sure. I'll even read you what's written on it."

CHILD: Here comes Charley back.

BEATRICE: *flourishing an ampty can of Bon Ami cleaning powder* Come on, let's go up to the attic. And I'll read it to you. It's all about this little chicken. See him? He's just hatched out of the egg and he hasn't scratched yet.

DR. PROGRESSAURUS' STUDENTS race off.

DR. HISTORY'S STUDENTS run in with a long piece of rope.

DR. HISTORY: Now children, what do you call this rope?

DR. HISTORY'S STUDENTS: We call this rope time. All of time.

DR. HISTORY: All that we know of time. Very well.
Today, children, we are going to decorate this rope. And
I've given you each little bits of coloured thread which
I want you to tie on at certain places. Tie a red ribbon
where B.C. ends, Jacob. That's right. Now tie a purple
thread where Socrates is killed, Mary. A little closer to
Jacob's thread, dear. Now, Samuel, tie your orange
thread at the point where many people think man first
appeared on earth. Right! And now, Bruno, tie your
white thread for the end of the Azoic period. Good.
Alfred, tie a thread where the provinces of Canada are
confederated. Good. Now David, tie your thread where
Byzantium falls to the Turks in 1453. So — now — lift up
the time rope. Children, do you see what a great deal
of space is here before man arrives on the scene?

CHILD: The dinosaurs were instead of us. Are we really
descended from dinosaurs, Miss History?

DR. HISTORY: I once met a man who I'm quite sure
was. But the greater danger is that we're turning into
dinosaurs. Very well. Let us break off. You may talk
and play for five minutes.

*She retires and examines the globe, spinning it, while her
STUDENTS chatter and skip with the time-rope.*

DR. HOSTRY: *returning to the STUDENTS*   What I
wish we could do with time. Now for the rest of our
history lesson. Let us now do: KINGS AND EMPERORS.

CHILD: Please, Hilda, can we do the Roman Empire?

DR. HISTORY: Come here, my child.   *She smacks her
on the hand.*   Let that be a lesson to you never to call
me by my first name.

CHILD: Ow! Oh dear, I'm awfully sorry, Miss History.
    But could we do the Roman Empire?

DR. HISTORY: Wouldn't you rather do the Chinese
    Empire?

DR. HISTORY'S STUDENTS: Ming! Chang! Ping!

CHILD: No, we wanta do —

THE DECLINE AND FALL OF THE ROMAN EMPIRE
OR
A LESSON FROM HISTORY IN HISTORY

*This sequence needs further research and explanation,
preferably by the Classics teacher and his/her students. The
pronunciation and spelling alone might take a day to check
out. Think up mimes that fit the most prominent names —
for example, the wolf who suckled Romulus and Remus
can be made out of a gymnastic combination of three bodies.
Use small-sized actors for the ancestral sucklers. As long as
the rhythm of the play is not lost, there is a great deal of
interpretation and improvisation possible here with big
moments of assassinations and poisonings; diminuendos
towards the fall.*

DR. HISTORY'S STUDENTS:

Romulus!	Romulus	et Remus	et Lupa
Titus Tatius		Numa Pompilius	Tarquinius Priscus
		Tarquin!	
Res	Publica	Senatus	Populusque

ROMAE

Hannibal	Scipio	Publius	Cornelius
Sulla	Latifundi	Minifundi	Gracchi!
Marius	Pompey	Cicero	and Caesar
Julius Caesar!		Julius Caesar!	Julius — Brutus!
		Antony et Cleopatra!	

AUGUSTUS

Augustus Tiberius   Caligula Claudius!
Nero Vespasian   Titus Domitian!
Nerva Trajan   Termini Termini
Termini termini termini termini TERMINI
Hadrian Antonius Pius Marcus Aurelius
Unum centum   sexegesima unum
Gloria glorissima   gloria glorissimus!
Commodus Septimus   Severus Alexander
Caracalla   Macrinus Elogabalus
Max iminus   Pupienus et Balbinus
     Philip the Arab!

Decius Gallus   Aemilianus and Valerian
Gallienus Claudius   Quintillus et Aurelian
Tacitus Probus Carus Carinus et Numerian
Diocletian   Constantius

CONSTANTINE

Julian Jovian   Valentinian Honorius
     Valentinian
     the Third
Maximus Avitus   Marjorian Severus
Anthemus Olybrius   Glycerius Julius Negros

ROMULUS

Romulus
Romulus Augustulus
Sic transit gloria Romael Romulus
Romulus! Romulus et Remus et Lupa!

*DR. HISTORY and her STUDENTS exit as DR.
PROGRESSAURUS enters with his STUDENTS for
their geography lesson.*

DR. PROGRESSAURUS: *carrying a red flag*   Now,
today, children, we are going to have our first lesson in
what is called Social Studies.

BEATRICE: Excuse me, Dr. Progressaurus, but didn't that used to be called History and Geography?

DR. PROGRESSAURUS: Beatrice. In Social Studies, we learn about lands and we learn about the people who live in those lands. Now I want the girls to take the sand on the beach here and make it into a heap so that you have a ditch that goes in a circle. We are going to make a model of a kind of land that many people live in. Boys, go down to the water and fill your sand pails with water.

BRUCE: I don't want to.

DR. PROGRESSAURUS: Raise your hands all those who want to continue with the lesson. *They all do except the boy.* You must go along with the majority, Bruce. That is what we call a democracy.

BRUCE: I still don't want to.

DR. PROGRESSAURUS: Why, Bruce?

BRUCE: Because I don't.

DR. PROGRESSAURUS: Then you'll feel awfully alone, Bruce. Good girls. Just a lovely heap of sand. Now — pour in the water, boys.

BEATRICE: Oh, I know. This is a lesson about land forms. We're going to find out what —

DR. PROGRESSAURUS: *clapping a hand over her mouth* Please Beatrice. I want the class to find out for themselves. You're always ruining lessons this way. You'll tell them what it is before they find out what it is. So I'll just have to put this bandage around your mouth. *He gags her.* Now children. Is the heap of sand the girls made completely surrounded by the water the boys brought in their pails?

DR. PROGRESSAURUS' STUDENTS: Yes.

DR. PROGRESSAURUS: Very well then. Now, we're going off on a walk by the water. We'll always keep by the water and I'll put this small red flag in the sand here. Yes — we won't need the model we made, Bruce. We've got a much larger model. *He chuckles.*   You do quite right to kick the heap of sand the girls made — we've got a much, much larger model. By the way, how many of you think we'll see the red flag again if we keep walking in one direction along the water?

DR. PROGRESSAURUS' STUDENTS: *some shaking their heads, others saying yes*   "No. We'll never see it again. Yes! We will."

BEATRICE goes into a mute frenzy of sign language.

DR. PROGRESSAURUS: Now we'll just find out, shall we? Oh golly, this is going to be a perfect lesson. I'll write it up and send it in for possible publication to the *Teacher of Tomorrow* Magazine. Goodbye, little red flag.

DR. PROGRESSAURUS' STUDENTS: Goodbye, little red flag.

As they go off, the noise diminishes. But BRUCE darts back to take the flag.

Now the noise crescendoes as they come round the island and enter again on the opposite side of the stage.

DR. PROGRESSAURUS: Now kids — here's — well, I guess the little red flag is just a bit further on than I thought.

Furious gestures from BEATRICE.

DR. PROGRESSAURUS: Yes, I know — but I don't think that is the heap of sand we made with the — water — Bruce would go and kick it, of course — I'm not blaming you, Bruce. You should follow your natural playful instincts. Come on, kids, we'll find that flag yet.

BRUCE: Charley. How can we find the flag if we keep on walking away from it?

DR. PROGRESSAURUS: That's a very good question, Bob. But you see I've a hunch that there's some way this piece of land we live in will bring us — after a while — closer again to the little red flag we left behind us. Come on, kids. Let's keep on walking.

As they exit once again, BRUCE now puts up the flag again and BEATRICE sees him.

DR. PROGRESSAURUS: No, Beatrice. You may not take your mouth gag off.

Their noise fades out.

Just as their noise fades in again BRUCE gallops in and cabbages the flag. BEATRICE fights him for it, but he wins and he puts the flag behind him.

DR. PROGRESSAURUS: Well, kids, this I — oops is bigger than I thought. We'll just have to keep on. Say, Beatrice. What are you trying to tell me? By golly Bruce. You picked up the flag and you put it in your pocket. That was very aggressive, Bruce, and shows hostility. Well — put the flag down, Bruce. So we walked and walked along the water and we came back to where we started from. What do we call that, I wonder?

DR. PROGRESSAURUS' STUDENTS: The land where we live.

BRUCE: Charley. We've walked all the way round a lake.

DR. PROGRESSAURUS: No, Bruce. We didn't.

BRUCE: Well we could reach the flag again if we walked around a lake.

DR. PROGRESSAURUS: We're in a lake, but —

BRUCE: You see —

DR. PROGRESSAURUS: Well leave that flag there and we'll just walk around the beach once more. Come on.

A Marx Brothers' routine.

DR. PROGRESSAURUS: *shouting from offstage*   The water completely surrounds us! It's a lake. We've just run round a lake! Hands up! How many believe in me rather than Bruce?

Some hands go up.

BRUCE: The majority believe in me, Charley.

DR. PROGRESSAURUS: All right, Beatrice. Take off your gag and vote!

She raises her hand.

BRUCE: It's still a draw!

BEATRICE: No, it is not. We live on an island. An island is a piece of land completely surrounded by water.

BRUCE: Prove it!

BEATRICE: I can't prove this place is an island if you won't believe that it is. You still think the world is flat.

BRUCE: All right. Now, how many think we live on an island?

All raise hands. Eventually, even BRUCE.

DR. PROGRESSAURUS: Isn't this wonderful. This is the way a democracy should work. Now it's time, kids, for your "do what you like" break. Thank you, Beatrice. You brought in the word "island" at just the right moment.

They fade off.

LANGUAGES

See page 309 of Cours Moyen. *In this sequence, have a French teacher fill in the correct phonetic symbols, as well as the proper accents, and rehearse the STUDENTS. Play with the sounds.*

DR. PROGRESSAURUS' STUDENTS:
    (i) !   ici, île, bicyclette.
    (e) !   école, donner, allez.
    (   ) !   tête, merci, neige, avec.

    i i i i i
    e e e e

    (a) !   madame!
    (a) !   pas! passer.
    (   ) !   joli restaurant!
    (o)   jour où.

    a o u u!
    u u u u u u!

(Y) !   rue
(   ) !   bleu
(œ) !   oeuf
(c) !   ce

œ œ œ œ œ œ

DR. HISTORY and her STUDENTS enter.

LANGUAGES II

DR. HISTORY'S STUDENTS: *speaking rapidly*
Nouns!
First Declension!
Singular

Nominative	porta
Accusative	portam!
Genitive	portae
Dative	portae
Ablative	porta
Vocative	porta

Plural!

Portae   portas   portarum   portis   portis   portae!

Verbs!
VOCO!

Passive!	Imperfect!	Indicative!
vocabar		vocabaris
vocabatur		vocabatur
vocabamur		vocabamini
vocabantur		vocabantur

Vocabantur,   vocabantur,   vocabantur VOCO!

LANGUAGES III

The first two verses of "My Bonnie" in Latin; perhaps with rhythm and instruments.

DR. PROGRESSAURUS' STUDENTS:
Trans aequora abiit Chloe;
Abest Chloe longissime:
Trans aequora abiit Chloe;
Reddatur amata Chloe.
Reddas, reddas, O reddas amatam mihi.

O Zephyre, aequore perfla;
Oventi, perflate mare;
O Zephyre, aequore perfla;
Ut mihi reddatur Chloe.

LANGUAGES IV

Let yourself go. Look at the first choruses in Names and Nicknames *for ideas.*

DR. HISTORY'S STUDENTS:
GRAMMAR!

Bare subject	Bare Predicate	Bare Object
The boy	hit	the boy.

Transitional Expressions

Addition:	moreover, further, furthermore, again
Subtraction:	but, yet, nevertheless, still, however
Contrast:	on the other hand, on the one hand on the contrary
Coincidence:	equally important, meanwhile, in the meantime, at the same time, at the same place
Purpose:	for this purpose, to this end, with this object.

| Result: | hence, accordingly, consequently, thus |
| Summary: | in sum, to sum up, on the whole, in brief. |

DR. PROGRESSAURUS' STUDENTS:

Adjectives to Express Yourself With:

Maroon	angry	mild	calm
Pale	brilliant	bright	sparkling
Dark	darkling	belligerent	malevolent
Sylvan	singular	candid	autumnal.

DR. HISTORY: Alfred. Name as many causes of the First World War as you have discovered from your reading in the library.

ALFRED:

Some Causes of the First World War Are:

ONE	Archduke Ferdinand's assassination.
TWO	Alsace-Lorraine.
THREE	Militarism.
FOUR	Trade rivalry.
FIVE	Nationalism.
SIX	Turkey — the Sick Man of Europe.

DR. HISTORY'S STUDENTS march out as the reasons are being chanted.

DR. PROGRESSAURUS: Now, boys and girls. For this past month we have been living in France.

BRUCE: Je ne veux pas.

DR. PROGRESSAURUS: We have cooked French food.
    The STUDENTS react to this.   We have talked French.
    They react again.   We have re-enacted many scenes
    from French history — the triumph of the Romans over
    the Gauls.   *There is a scream.*   St. Bartholomew's
    Massacre.   *There is another scream!*   What episode
    will we re-enact today?

DR. PROGRESSAURUS' STUDENTS: The Revolution!

BRUCE: And Charley, you'll be King Louis Seize.

DR. PROGRESSAURUS' STUDENTS: *as they crown him*
    Louis Seize Louis Seize Louis Seize.

*He is left alone on an improvised throne while the class
retreat muttering to one corner.*

DR. PROGRESSAURUS' STUDENTS:
    Saint Antoine Corvée corvée corvée
    Pas de pain pas de pain pas de pain pas de pain.

*There is much muttering of these words suddenly boiling
over into an attack on some chairs which become
the Bastille. Some of the STUDENTS turn the chairs upside
down and whirl them around over their heads.*

DR. PROGRESSAURUS' STUDENTS:

Bastille!	Quatorze juillet.	Quatorze juillet.
Aux armes citoyens		Où est le roi?
A bas les aristos.		Madame la
		guillotine
Liberté	fraternité	égalité
Nettoyez les aristos.		

They seize DR. PROGRESSAURUS and lead him up the scaffold. He makes gestures to them.

DR. PROGRESSAURUS: "Ma peuple."

The STUDENTS murmur.

DR. PROGRESSAURUS' STUDENTS: Chop!

The executioner lifts up a wastepaper basket as Louis Seize's head. DR. PROGRESSAURUS rises rather shakily.

DR. PROGRESSAURUS: Now, boys and girls, what lesson do we learn from the French Revolution?

BEATRICE: That democracy doesn't work too well.

DR. PROGRESSAURUS: No, no, no. What do we learn, boys and girls?

DR. PROGRESSAURUS' STUDENTS: Kings are bad, Charley. Democracy is best.

DR. HISTORY and her STUDENTS enter.

A GEOMETRY LESSON
TERMS AND DEFINITIONS

This is really a ballet.

DR. HISTORY'S STUDENTS:
    Acute angle   axiom   arc of a circle
    Hypotenuse   Hypothesis
    Incommensurable magnitudes
    Isosceles triangle: A triangle having two equal sides
    Rhombus   Rhombus Rhombus Rhombus:
                         a quadrilateral in which the four
                         sides are equal.

Book Three: Proposition Three

To:	Circumscribe a circle about a triangle
Given:	ABC is a triangle
Required:	To circumscribe a circle about ABC
Construction:	Draw the right bisectors of BC and AC, intersecting at O. Join OA. With centre O and radius OA describe a circle. This circle passes through A, B and C.
Proof:	Join OB, OC. O lies on the right bisector of BC, OB = OC
Similarly:	OC = OA OB = OC = OA And the circle passes through A, B and C.
Question:	Is it always possible to circumscribe a circle about a given quadrilateral?

Again, play around with Euclid.

A CHEMISTRY LESSON

DR. PROGRESSAURUS' STUDENTS: *coughing as if gas masked; explosives and lightness vs. heaviness can be suggested.*

Table of the Elements

Hydrogen	Copper
Helium	Zinc
Carbon	Arsenic
Nitrogen	Silver, Tin
Oxygen	Antimony
Fluorine	Iodine
Neon	Gold
Sodium	Mercury
Magnesium	Lead
Aluminum	Lead
Silicon	Bismuth
Phosphorus	Radium
Sulphur	Uranium
Chlorine	Americium
Calcium	Curium
Iron	Berkelium
Cobalt	*Californium*
Nickel	Canadium?

DR. PROGRESSAURUS enters with a crutch and a telescope.

DR. PROGRESSAURUS: Now boys and girls, yesterday we conducted Galileo's experiment at the Leaning Tower of Pisa in which you managed to drop an iron ball on my foot.

BRUCE: But it fell just as fast as the bale of feathers.

DR. PROGRESSAURUS: I know. But next time — try to hit my foot with the feathers. Today, following in Galileo's footsteps, how would you like to study the moon through a telescope?

BRUCE: *already looking through a telescope*   Charley, there's a strange thing on the moon. I think it's an elephant.

DR. PROGRESSAURUS: Why so there is. Whatever can be the matter?

They all shade their eyes and stare directly at the moon.

BEATRICE: I think I've found the difficulty, Dr. Progressaurus. Come and look at this end of the telescope.

DR. PROGRESSAURUS: Why — someone — somehow a mouse has got down the telescope.

As he reaches in, the mouse climbs up his sleeve and there is a chaotic exodus.

DR. PROGRESSAURUS: Help! Help!

POETRY

DR. HISTORY'S STUDENTS:
"The Hummingbird"
by Emily Dickinson

A Route of Evanescence
With a revolving Wheel —
A Resonance of Emerald —
A Rush of Cochineal —
And every Blossom on the Bush
Adjusts it's tumbled Head —
The mail from Tunis, probably,
An easy Morning's Ride —

DR. PROGRESSAURUS' STUDENTS: *à la The Fugs?*
"The Tyger"
by William Blake

Tyger! Tyger! burning bright
In the forests of the night,
What immortal hand or eye
Could frame thy fearful symmetry?

In what distant deeps or skies
Burned the fire of thine eyes?
On what wings dare he aspire?
What the hand dare seize the fire?

And what shoulder, and what art,
Could twist the sinews of thy heart?
And when thy heart began to beat,
What dreadful hand? and what dread feat?

What the hammer? what the chain?
In that furnace was thy brain?
What the anvil? what dread grasp
Dare its deadly terrors clasp?

When the stars threw down their spears,
And watered heaven with their tears,
Did he smile his work to see?
Did he who made the Lamb make thee?

Tyger! Tyger! burning bright
In the forests of the night,
What immortal hand or eye,
Dare frame thy fearful symmetry?

DR. PROGRESSAURUS: Very well, boys and girls.
You may do what you like until suppertime. If any of
you want to drive the cars around the race track just
feel free to do so. Beatrice, you're very poor at driving.
You should get out and practice more.

BEATRICE: I don't want to learn to drive. I might
kill somebody, including myself.

DR. PROGRESSAURUS: Poor Beatrice. You'll never get
adjusted to our modern world.

BEATRICE: I don't want to get adjusted to it. It's 80%
hideous.

BRUCE: Leave her alone, Charley.

*As DR. PROGRESSAURUS fades away, they all wait till
he's really gone — then . . .*

BRUCE: Okay, Beatrice. Where are the new lessons?

BEATRICE: I'm amazed you're anxious to see them, Bruce. Since you can't read them. The cook, Mrs. Smith was able to get us the whole correspondence lessons for Grade XII Physics. They came in the mail this morning to her from the Department of Education. *She begins handing out papers.*   So we can get going at studying them.

GIRL: Has the little chicken who hasn't scratched yet appeared in a dream to you lately, Beatrice?

BEATRICE produces a battered Bon Ami can. The STUDENTS all crane forward to look at it.

BEATRICE: Yes, he appeared last night.

BOY: Tell us what he told you. Can you?

BEATRICE: We're soon going to leave this island. On a boat!

DR. PROGRESSAURUS' STUDENTS: Leave? On a boat?

BEATRICE: We're going to be given an examination. It's most important that we do well. And we'll meet another set of young people who've been brought up the way we have.

GIRL: Will the little chicken still care for us?

BEATRICE: Of course. He couldn't leave us now. He's all we've got. How could we have lived without him loving us? Let's repeat his worship as we go down to the woods to do our Physics problems.

They recite the contents of a Bon Ami can, the French being favoured.

DR. PROGRESSAURUS' STUDENTS:
  Nettoyez la vaisselle
  Nettoyez la vaisselle.

Their chant fades off.

DR. HISTORY enters with her STUDENTS.

DR. HISTORY: Now — scholars, young men, young women, ladies and gentlemen — this is our farewell dance at the school, for tomorrow we go east on the train to meet your benefactor. In a way, you will meet the world for the first time although it also will meet you. Remember that. Now — dance and enjoy yourselves. You have reached the end of what they used to call when I was a girl — Middle School.

Her STUDENTS dance — precisely and beautifully.

The scene switches to a choatic "Twist" at DR. PROGRESS-AURUS' school, then back to DR. HISTORY'S STUDENTS.

The scene fades away and we are ready for The Judgment.

MR. FROTHINGALE and the GOVERNOR-GENERAL walk along the empty stage as if on a terrace. The GOVERNOR-GENERAL is an incredibly distinguished old man who carries a cane and wears medals.

MR. FROTHINGALE: Your Excellency, you've no idea how pleased I am that you could come to judge the results of this experiment.

GOVERNOR-GENERAL: But, Frothingale, the pleasure is just about all mine. I too have longed to know which system of education was better. How incredibly enlightened of you to have given two such fanatics as Miss History and Dr. Progressaurus a chance to prove their stuff — ten baby orphans apiece.

MR. FROTHINGALE: By the way, before they arrive, what method of judgment will you use?

GOVERNOR-GENERAL: Well, I'll see them as a group at the garden party. But then I would like to have personal interviews. I'll choose the persons completely at random. I should also like some sort of social situation set up. Why not a tea pot with some tea in it and cups and saucers? So often character is revealed in little things like table manners.

A tea table is set up. DR. HISTORY and DR. PROGRESS-AURUS enter for the judgment.

MR. FROTHINGALE: Why my dear Miss History. And my dear Dr. Progressaurus. How are you after all these years?   *Silence.*   Goodness gracious. What have I done to you? Have they made you mute?

DR. HISTORY: *laughing*   No indeed, Mr. Frothingale. But it is eighteen years since I've seen you.

MR. FROTHINGALE: And you, Dr. Progressaurus. Can you still speak to me?

DR. PROGRESSAURUS: All righty. Golly, I was just waiting for the lady to speak first.

MR. FROTHINGALE: Well, I can hardly wait to see your products. Miss History's are to come in first. But before that — I must introduce you to His Excellency.

DR. HISTORY curtseys to the GOVERNOR-GENERAL and DR. PROGRESSAURUS bows.

GOVERNOR-GENERAL: And I am very pleased to meet you. Both of you have given up eighteen years to the worthiest of causes. By the way, before your students enter could you each tell me what you set out to accomplish with your children?

DR. PROGRESSAURUS: What I tried to do, Your Excellency, was to teach the child, not the subject. To teach them to express themselves. They were never forced to do a single thing they didn't want to.

DR. HISTORY: All I tried to do was give them an education.

GOVERNOR-GENERAL: I see. Well. Is this your group then, Miss History?

DR. HISTORY'S STUDENTS enter. They are blazered and quiet and neat. The one or two untidy souls are hardly noticeable. DR. HISTORY takes over His Excellency and MR. FROTHINGALE to introduce them, as well as DR. PROGRESSAURUS, to her STUDENTS. The scholars bow and curtsey. From the opposite side of the stage come DR. PROGRESSAURUS' STUDENTS. DR. HISTORY'S STUDENTS see them first — reaction — the grown-ups turn around and behold them too. All of them are individualists although there are several groups devoted to one brand of individualism. Some lumber, some slouch, some are dressed fit to kill with jewellery. BRUCE's transistor set blares. One girl twists her drum majorette's baton. The two groups confront each other. There is a silence.

One of DR. HISTORY'S STUDENTS, a boy, goes over to DR. PROGRESSAURUS and bites his finger. DR. PROGRESSAURUS screams "Ouch!"

BRUCE: Hey! Lookit, kids. Charley got bitten on the finger by one of them. They'll lose marks for that.

BOY: Oh I'm awfully sorry, sir. Miss History, I've no conception of why I did that. I apologize abjectly, Dr. Progressaurus. I don't know what got into me. Did I bite you badly?

DR. PROGRESSAURUS: It's perfectly okay. Just expressing yourself. Go to it. Here — try the other hand.

DR. HISTORY: When he was very small, Dr. Progressaurus — you may recall that Baby Number 7 bit you. I think Jerry is Baby Number 7. This doesn't justify his strange behaviour, of course.

DR. PROGRESSAURUS: Well — would you say Baby Number 7 has made progress or not, Hilda?

DR. HISTORY: Yes. With an interesting relapse.

GOVERNOR-GENERAL: Now, while the rest of you attend Mr. Frothingale's garden party in his large and capacious grounds, I should like to talk to some of you. *He consults a list of names.* Beatrice and Bruce from this group. And Stephen and Cynthia from this group. One at a time. Cynthia first.

MR. FROTHINGALE: Let's see which group can run the fastest. Down to the goldfish pond and back.

They all disappear save the GOVERNOR-GENERAL and CYNTHIA.

GOVERNOR-GENERAL: Pray be seated, my dear. Do you mind if I ask you a few questions?

CYNTHIA: No. But do please ask them.

GOVERNOR-GENERAL: Only a few. That's what I'm here for.

CYNTHIA: Have you had your tea yet, Your Excellency?

GOVERNOR-GENERAL: No, I haven't.

CYNTHIA: Perhaps you'd like me to pour it for you then.

GOVERNOR-GENERAL: Why that would be very pleasant.

CYNTHIA: And how do you take your tea?

GOVERNOR-GENERAL: Why, my dear, you've asked me more questions than I have of you.

CYNTHIA: Only one more.

GOVERNOR-GENERAL: I take it clear, Cynthia.   *She pours him some tea.*   Cynthia, what's the saddest thing that ever happened to you at Miss History's school?

CYNTHIA: One of us took ill and died six years ago. We all liked him very much. That was heartbreaking.

GOVERNOR-GENERAL: Yes. And what was the happiest thing that happened to you at Miss History's school?

CYNTHIA: When I began to like my music lessons.

GOVERNOR-GENERAL: You didn't at first?

CYNTHIA: At first I had temper tantrums, but I got over them. With help. And then suddenly they couldn't get me away from the piano.

GOVERNOR-GENERAL: Would you like to play for me, Cynthia?

CYNTHIA: Yes.

She goes to the piano and plays a short piece.

GOVERNOR-GENERAL: Thank you, Cynthia. You may tell Bruce to come in now.

CYNTHIA curtseys and then retires.

BRUCE: *striding forward*   Hi!

GOVERNOR-GENERAL: Good day to you, Bruce. What's that you're listening to?

BRUCE: Gee. Is that thing on? Music.

He turns off the transistor set.

GOVERNOR-GENERAL: And what are you eating?

BRUCE: I'm not eating. I'm chewing gum.

GOVERNOR-GENERAL: I see, Bruce. Who was the first Prime Minister of Canada?

BRUCE: How would I know? You?

GOVERNOR-GENERAL: You live in Canada, don't you?

BRUCE: Do I? I never could figure that out. You know something? It was finally proven to me that I'd been living on an island all these years. Charley made the captain sail the boat all the way around it. Course, it still could have been a trick.

GOVERNOR-GENERAL: Who is this Charley?

BRUCE: The guy that teaches us.

GOVERNOR-GENERAL: Oh. Dr. Progressaurus. Bruce —
I've mislaid my glasses. What does this fine printing say?

BRUCE: You got me there, Gov. I can't neither read or
write.

GOVERNOR-GENERAL: I beg your pardon.

BRUCE: Go ahead. Beg it. I'll give it back. You see, I
never wanted to learn.

GOVERNOR-GENERAL: But how on earth did you get
into Grade Twelve?

BRUCE: Charley always said it'd hurt my feelings if I
failed. So it would have.   *He imitates crying.*
Anyways Beatrice reads the exam questions to me. And
my memory's pretty good. Ask me the date of any big
battle there's ever been.

GOVERNOR-GENERAL: Actium!

BRUCE: *giving its date*   You see? These days, I figure
you don't need to read or write. Just press a button.
Know your traffic signals. If you wanna book — get a
record.

GOVERNOR-GENERAL: Suppose you wanted to write
a love letter?

BRUCE: Get Beatrice to write it for me. Or send her a
tape.

GOVERNOR-GENERAL: I see. And are you happy?

BRUCE: Happy? Sometimes. Other times. It's that
    Beatrice. I'd be quite happy chewing gum and listening
    to my transistor set if she didn't keep saying I was going
    to turn to stone. I keep feeling my ankles to make sure.

GOVERNOR-GENERAL: Well. I guess that's all, Bruce.
    On your way out could you tell Stephen to come in.
    Good Heavens! What are you doing?

BRUCE balances the tea pot on his head.

BRUCE: Hey Steve. Come in and see me balance the
    tea jug.

STEPHEN enters and takes the tea pot off BRUCE's head.

STEPHEN: Would you like some more tea, Your
    Excellency?

GOVERNOR-GENERAL: No. Could I pour you some
    though?

STEPHEN: Why yes, that would be very nice. I — I take
    it clear, sir.

GOVERNOR-GENERAL: What do you think of Dr.
    Progressaurus' students?

STEPHEN: I have an opinion, but I'm keeping it to
    myself if you don't mind.

GOVERNOR-GENERAL: By the way, I see my shoe has
    come untied. Would you mind tying it up for me?

STEPHEN: I'm sorry, Your Excellency, but I always
    think a man should tie up his own shoes.

GOVERNOR-GENERAL: *at first angry, reaching for his cane, then* — Why — as a matter of fact, it *is* tied. Must be an optical illusion. Do you ever play at Miss History's school? Or do you just work, work, work all the time?

STEPHEN: Actually we pretty well do what we like. To work is to play.

GOVERNOR-GENERAL: Ah, you've been brainwashed.

STEPHEN: Yes. I suppose we have.

GOVERNOR-GENERAL: What's your favourite pastime?

STEPHEN: Whist.

GOVERNOR-GENERAL: Whist?

STEPHEN: You know — the card game. I could play it day and night. I like mathematics. By the way, could I disagree with you?

GOVERNOR-GENERAL: *stiffly* Perhaps.

STEPHEN: When you said we'd been brainwashed at Miss History's class, that's just not so. You have to do something with your mind. It all depends on what *kind* of water you wash it in.

GOVERNOR-GENERAL: *rising in a pretended fury* Do you dare to disagree with the titular ruler of your country?

STEPHEN: *pausing and backing up* Yes! When it comes to slurring my teacher I'll disagree with anybody.

GOVERNOR-GENERAL: *laughing*   Good, Stephen.
    You may go now and tell Beatrice to come in.

*BEATRICE enters. Her clothes are a cross between the wild
and the blazer philosophy.*

BEATRICE: What's been going on in here, Your
    Excellency? I heard raised voices. Oh dear — before I
    forget.´

She curtseys.

GOVERNOR-GENERAL: And who taught you to do
    that?

BEATRICE: No one really, except I'm, as they say,
    playing this by ear.

GOVERNOR-GENERAL: Now, Beatrice, what do you
    think about life in general?

BEATRICE: Dear me. I didn't know the examination was
    going to be so tough. Well, here goes. If it weren't for the
    little chick who hasn't scratched yet it'd be unbearable.

The GOVERNOR-GENERAL is silent.

BEATRICE: You look sort of stunned.

GOVERNOR-GENERAL: I imagine I do. You see, most
    young ladies I know would say — "God" at this point.

BEATRICE: Okay. God sends the little chicken. Bon
    Ami. Here he is.   *She shows him the Bon Ami can.*
    I found him years ago on a trash heap and then he started
    to appear to me in dreams.

GOVERNOR-GENERAL: You've made a whole religion out of an empty can of household cleansing powder?!

BEATRICE: I guess we have. But we had to do something. You see where it says "good for cleaning windows." It doesn't just mean windows.

GOVERNOR-GENERAL: It doesn't?

BEATRICE: No. It means the windows of the soul. The little chick washes them for you and hasn't scratched yet.

GOVERNOR-GENERAL: And do all the rest of you believe in this old tin can?

BEATRICE: More or less. You see Dr. Progressaurus wouldn't let us believe in him, so. . . .

GOVERNOR-GENERAL: Some of you did remarkably well on your Grade Twelve examinations. Wasn't Dr. Progressaurus responsible for that?

BEATRICE: No. Little Chick was. He appeared to me in a dream and told me to get the cook to send away for the correspondence lessons. Everyone studied hard because they wanted to please the little chick who hasn't scratched yet.

GOVERNOR-GENERAL: I see. By the way, are all the orphan children who went to Pelee Island with Dr. Progressaurus still in the group?

BEATRICE: The eagles carried Florrie away.

GOVERNOR-GENERAL: The eagles carried Florrie away! Good heavens! What did Dr. Progressaurus do about that?

BEATRICE: Florrie always had wanted to be an eagle. So he figured it was all right.

GOVERNOR-GENERAL: Did you ever miss anything on the island?

BEATRICE: Yes. Someone to rebel against. Charley always gave in too easily.

GOVERNOR-GENERAL: What do you want the rest of your life to be like?

BEATRICE: *dreamily*   I wrote a poem about it. When I was fourteen. It's a chant poem we all say together. Would you like to hear it?

As she begins the poem, her group comes in to do it with her and all the others appear also.

ALL:
Existence gives to me.
What does he give to me?

He gives to me: a pebble
He gives to me: a dewdrop
He gives to me: a piece of string
He gives to me: a straw

Pebble dewdrop piece of string straw

The pebble is a huge dark hill I must climb
The dewdrop is a great storm lake that we must cross
The string is a road that I cannot find
The straw is a sign whose meaning I forget

Hill lake road sign

ALL:
    But love and patience do quite change the scene
    The desert fades into meadows pleasant and green
    The mountain becomes a pebble in my hand
    The lake calms down to a dewdrop on a flower
    The weary road is a string around your wrist
    The mysterious sign is a straw that whistles "Home"

    Pebble dewdrop piece of string straw

MR. FROTHINGALE: Well, Your Excellency. Have you made up your mind which school wins?

GOVERNOR-GENERAL: No, I haven't. I shall just have to walk around a bit till my mind clears.

He walks around — lost for a few moments in the crowd.

GOVERNOR-GENERAL: A difficult decision. Oh, a difficult decision.

DR. HISTORY: My dear. What is that curious bracelet you're wearing?

GIRL: It's all that's left of my beddy-bye blanket I had when I was a baby. I don't feel secure unless I have it by me.

DR. HISTORY: Why don't you let me keep it for you? It looks rather — shabby and scruffy, don't you think?

GIRL: Okay. Gee. Gee, I think I feel much better now.

DR. HISTORY: Yes. And I'll always keep it for you here. Right in my purse.

GIRLS: Shame on Bruce. He can't read. He's a non-reading Grade Twelve graduate. Yah, yah, yah Brucie!

BRUCE: Hilda, your girls are teasing me because I can't read.

GIRLS: Poor old Bruce. He can't read the street signs.

DR. HISTORY: The first step, Bruce, is a simple one. What is my name so far as you are concerned?

BRUCE: Uh – Miss History?

OTHERS: Beatrice! Look what we found at a store at the bottom of Mr. Frothingale's garden? Twenty cans of Bon Ami cleansing powder with Little Chick's picture on every one of them!

They sprinkle the powder.

GOVERNOR-GENERAL: It's a tie. But incredible luck for you, Progressaurus, it's a tie. And there's going to be a tie-breaker.

MR. FROTHINGALE: Oh, how glorious. The experiment can go on. Never fear. Frothingale Breweries made an immense profit last year.

GOVERNOR-GENERAL: How I propose to break the tie is in the following way: Miss History – Dr. Progressaurus, you will exchange your groups for the final year of their high school education.

DR. HISTORY'S STUDENTS: No. No.

GOVERNOR-GENERAL: Miss History — you will go to
   Pelee Island and what you must do to these poor
   progressively maladjusted mites is change them without
   changing what is charming about them — about some
   of them. Progressaurus, you will go out to the prairies
   and superintend this group. If you're any good at all
   they'll have changed you by the time a year is up. Then
   in a year's time we shall see.

DR. HISTORY faints.

ALL: It's too much for her. You've killed her. Irregular
   verbs. Irregular verbs.

GOVERNOR-GENERAL: No, no, no. She's made of
   sterner stuff than that. I'd faint myself in her situation.
   You see, Progressaurus, it's Beatrice who saved your
   skin and made it a draw.

DR. PROGRESSAURUS: Beatrice! Why, she's my worst
   student.

GOVERNOR-GENERAL: No. She's your best. And she
   could, probably, have flourished only with your kind of
   neglect.

DR. PROGRESSAURUS: Stuff and nonsense. Boy, have
   I got my work cut out for me. Teaching you little snobs
   to be yourselves.

DR. HISTORY: *rising*   I think that's what made me
   swoon. The idea that he'd get them. But no — I'm not
   afraid. You can't make a sow's ear out of a silk purse —
   even you, Progressaurus, cannot effect *that* miracle. So,
   yes, I'll let you have my scholars.

BRUCE: *on bended knee*   Oh Miss History — please!
   Teach me how to read.

Appendix

A Liturgy

Bon Ami
Polishes as it cleans
Makes porcelain gleam
Ne rougit pas les mains.

Mode D'Emploi
Directions

No Red Hands.
Nettoie les fenêtres
N'a pas encore égratiné
Hasn't scratched yet.

Polie tout en nettoyant.

Use this for the religious scene with the children on the island.

TALONBOOKS — THEATRE FOR THE YOUNG 1978

Raft Baby — Dennis Foon
The Windigo — Dennis Foon
Heracles — Dennis Foon
A Chain of Words — Irene Watts
Apple Butter — James Reaney
Geography Match — James Reaney
Names and Nicknames — James Reaney
Ignoramus — James Reaney
A Teacher's Guide to Theatre for Young People —
    Jane Baker, ed.
A Mirror of Our Dreams — Joyce Doolittle and Zina Barnieh